Flea Market Jewelry

Flea Market Jewelry

New Style from Old Treasures

Binky Morgan

Sterling Publishing Co., Inc. New York
A Sterling/Chapelle Book

Chapelle Ltd.

Owner: Jo Packham

Editor: Linda Orton

Staff: Areta Bingham, Kass Burchett, Marilyn Goff, Holly Hollingsworth, Susan Jorgensen, Barbara Milburn, Karmen Quinney, Cindy Stoeckl, Sara Toliver, Kim Taylor, Kristi Torsak

Photography: Kevin Dilley, for Hazen Imaging, Inc.
Scot Zimmerman for Scot Zimmerman Photography

Library of Congress Cataloging-in-Publication

Morgan, Binky.
    Flea market jewelry : new style from old treasures / Binky Morgan.
        p. cm.
    Includes index.
    ISBN 0-8069-2695-3
    1. Handicraft--Equipment and supplies. 2. Costume jewelry--Recycling.
3. Jewelry making. 4. Collectibles in interior decoration. 5. Artists'
materials. I. Title.

TT153.7.M67 2001
745-5--dc21   2001031436

10 9 8 7 6 5 4 3 2 1

A Sterling/Chapelle Book

Published by Sterling Publishing Company, Inc.
387 Park Avenue South, New York, NY 10016
© 2001 by Binky Morgan
Distributed in Canada by Sterling Publishing
⅘ Canadian Manda Group, One Atlantic Avenue, Suite 105
Toronto, Ontario, Canada M6K 3E7
Distributed in Great Britain and Europe by Cassell PLC
Wellington House, 125 Strand, London WC2R 0BB, England
Distributed in Australia by Capricorn Link (Australia) Pty Ltd.
P.O. Box 704, Windsor, NSW 2756, Australia
Printed in China
All Rights Reserved

Sterling ISBN 0-8069-2695-3

If you have any questions or comments, please contact:

Chapelle Ltd., Inc.
P.O. Box 9252
Ogden, UT 84409

Phone: (801) 621-2777
FAX: (801) 621-2788
e-mail: chapelle@chapelleltd.com
website: www.chapelleltd.com

Binky Morgan is a native Texan and lives in Austin, Texas, where she is the proprietress of Flashback—a vintage life-style store featuring jewelry, clothing, furniture, and all manner of objets d'art. Binky re-creates resurrected vintage clothing, along with her daughter Jesika and Jesika's best friend, Rachel.

Binky lives by the motto that "old is always better." Her interest in vintage items began at the age of sixteen when she started buying, then selling vintage clothing to vintage stores. She worked as a buyer for Homestead in Fredericksburg, Texas.

This book is dedicated to my daughter, Jesika Starr.

A special thanks to the following:
    Jimmy and Winnie J. Morgan
    Rachel Christopher
    Pinki Brewer
    David Upton for making the
    fringed leather bag pictured
    on page 58.

Table of Contents

Introduction

It always seems such a waste to throw away favored jewelry that has a broken clasp or a missing rhinestone; and what do you do with those pieces of jewelry that have been handed down from grandmother? Perhaps every time you go to the local thrift stores and flea markets, you see all those pieces of beautiful vintage jewelry and wonder what you could do with them. Well, I say, "if you love it—buy it!" If you uncover a lone earring, glue it to a glass ornament; or hang an old silver coffee urn lid upside down and place a candle in it. *Flea Market Jewelry* will show you how to resurrect vintage pieces of jewelry creatively with the wonderful projects and photographs included. The projects in this book will inspire you to create new jewelry from old, accent an overstuffed chair, embellish ornaments, and frame favored pictures or photographs.

When I was little I wore my mother's jewelry and it made me feel beautiful.

Eclectic Jewelry

Flea Market Jewelry can teach you to quickly turn your jewelry fantasies into realities. These are quick, easy, and inexpensive ideas that can change your wardrobe from ordinary to extraordinary.

We tend to forget that the simple, old, and sometimes discarded jeweled things in life can be redesigned, remade, and worn as if they were always a valued treasure. Such unique pieces of jewelry sometimes bring a sophisticated style, sometimes a funky twist, sometimes a contradiction to your usual daily wear, but all are considered part of a true eclectic vintage fashion.

Flea Markets

From London's legendary Portobello Road to every Saturday neighborhood garage sale, the flea market is the destination of choice for the savvy vintage shopper. *Flea Market Jewelry* celebrates the marriage of three great passions—jewelry, shopping, and making something yourself—and answers the important questions that lie behind every purchase, big or small, expensive or cheap, new or old, "What can I do with this and what will I wear it with?"

Literally, millions of shoppers every year spend free afternoons browsing through junk stores, flea markets, tag sales, and discount or thrift stores. Whether it be a few vendors set up in an oversized parking lot, an organized show offering booths from sellers across the country, or a street in an old town designated as antique row, these diverse markets provide an irresistible opportunity to search out hidden treasures.

Some such avid shoppers are fortunate enough to visit Europe's enticing old markets such as Portobello Road and Bermondsey in London, Porta Portnese in Rome, La Rastro in Madrid, and of course, Le Marche aux Puces in Paris. However, most of us tend to frequent the new indoor and outdoor "antique" fairs and tag sales that have proliferated on city streets and country roads.

This urge to acquire is hardly a recent phenomenon. Much like today's collectors, Renaissance shoppers sought out whatever they found beautiful. Whether it was old or new mattered less than it pleases the eye. Eventually, however, a valuable piece of jewelry was passed from one generation to the next and collecting became a serious business. Up until the end of World War I, collectors were those who invested in major expensive pieces of wearable finery. It was not until the end of World War II that collectors lightened up and collecting, as we know it, began. Although an antique by definition is considered to be an object at least a hundred years old, the term no longer refers to only fine jewelry, art, silver, porcelain, and furnishings. The items purchased by new collectors could be those that represented a simpler life; so gradually the line between antique and collectible became blurred and folksy objects were added to the mix.

People everywhere have taken to flea-market shopping with zeal, giving rise to an entire subculture of avid collectors who have turned shopping and collecting vintage flea-

market treasures into a national past time. New devotees are discovering the exhilaration, sociability, and pleasure of the chase each week. There is the lure of the hunt, the possibility that right up until the very last minute before closing time you might discover that very special treasure—one that no one else has.

There are other compelling reasons to get caught up in flea-market mania. With shoppers in every category looking for bargains, flea markets offer unbeatable prices in these days of discount shopping. With the advent of mass production, flea markets offer one-of-a-kind undeniably personal items that cannot be found on the shelves or in the catalogs of most department stores.

Flea Market Jewelry is written to show you how other collectors are using their finds, hoping to inspire you to shop with a more experienced eye, more imagination, and greater pleasure.

Jewelry Incidentals

Beading Fibers

Materials used for stringing beads or other jewelry findings are varied. Heavy beads work best when strung onto a substantial fiber such as heavy nylon, perle cotton, nylon monofilament (similar to fishing line) or multifilament rayon.

The shape or drape of a necklace or bracelet also determines the type of fiber used. Light silk or nylon thread (possibly doubled for strength) make a necklace that moves freely and drapes. A necklace that has a more defined shape or curve is best made from tiger-tail or nylon filament.

Leather, paper, and satin cording along with metallic wires are other materials that may be used for stringing beads or other jewelry findings.

In many cases, the thread or cording is stiff enough to slip through the hole in the bead without the use of a needle. A needle may be used for lighter weight fibers that spread apart; or another solution for these fibers is to tightly tape the end of the fibers together to form a "shoelace" tie that will pass through the hole.

Beading wire is best secured by twisting it around itself two or more times.

Jewelry Components

Head pins. These look much like nails, with one flat end that keeps the beads from falling off. Head pins come in a variety of gauges, finishes, and lengths. The narrowest and shorter head pins are ideal for small beads, while the larger gauge and lengths work well for drop crystals and larger beads.

The beads are strung onto the head pin and the excess is then cut with wire cutters, leaving ⅜" excess which is then formed into a loop with round-nosed or needle-nosed pliers.

Crimp beads. These are flattened or crimped with pliers to secure a looped end of tigertail, nylon filament, or cording onto a clasp or other jewelry component. It is important that the crimp bead is of the proper size to secure the material being used.

Jump rings. These are available in a wide range of sizes and finishes and are used to join clasps, beads, lengths of chain, drops, or other jewelry components.

Jump rings have a slight gap and should be opened side-to-side instead of being pulled straight apart so that they keep their circular shape and hold securely.

Open a jump ring or link like this.

Do not open a jump ring or link like this.

Fabric & Brooch Wrapping

Box or gift
Brooch or Pin
Fabric: vintage or scrap

This fabric was once a vintage gown.

1 Wrap the fabric around the box and pull the loose ends together at top of box, tucking raw edges under. Pin the brooch onto the excess fabric to secure and for decoration. *Note: Fabric may be cut with pinking shears for a decorative edge.*

Flea Market Shopping Tips:

• For the truly bargain-conscious and dedicated shopper, yard sales can provide the best opportunities to uncover an overlooked treasure. You may have to pick through more junk than at a flea market or antique shop, but prices will be lower since there is no middle-man involved and frequently owners are unaware of the value of certain items of which they have grown tired.

• Estate sales are a good source for finer pieces of jewelry. Because they are run by experts, you are unlikely to find a real bargain; however, you will still probably get a good value.

• Thrift and consignment shops are usually next in the hierarchy of pricing due to the large group of people—simplifying their lives—who do not have the time to organize a garage sale of their own. They take their pieces or have them picked up by these shops.

Jeweled Ornaments

Beading wire
Chain necklace
Epoxy
Fabric scissors
Glass globe ornament
Jewelry pieces (brooches, earrings,
   or necklace drops)
Needle-nosed pliers
Tape measure
Velvet fabric or ribbon (scrap)
Wire cutters

Make a stocking for the mantle from vintage fabric or clothing and a favorite pattern. Embellished ornaments are the perfect accent.

1 Remove the backs from the earrings and pins, and any other excess portions of jewelry pieces as necessary.

2 Glue the jewelry pieces onto the glass ornament as desired. *Note: Jewelry pieces may need to be bent slightly to follow the contour of the ornament before gluing.*

3 Cut one 1" x 6" velvet strip. Slip the velvet strip through the ornament loop and tie.

4 Attach the necklace chain to the ornament loop with beading wire.

Coffee Urn Lid Candleholder

Assorted beads
Beading thread
Beading wire
Candle
Coffee urn lid or other metal lid
Drill with small drill bits
Needle-nosed pliers
Plain and beaded chain necklaces (4)
Wire cutters

1 Drill sixteen holes at equal distances around the rim of lid.

2 Invert the lid to create candleholder. Attach each of the necklace chains to every fourth hole drilled in the lid, leaving a wire loop for attaching the beaded dangles.

3 String the beads as desired onto the beading thread and make sixteen beaded dangles. Attach the beaded dangles to the holes drilled around edge of lid.

4 Hang the candleholder and place candle inside. *Note: If a flammable decorative filler is used, it should be sprayed with a flame retardant. Burning candles should never be left unattended.*

Earring Push Pins

Pair of post earrings
Vintage beaded slippers

This pair of beaded slippers were too worn to wear, but still lovely to look at and could be used as accent pieces.

1 Attach the slippers to the wall, using earrings as push pins.
Note: The backings may be removed from clip earrings and a push pin or tack may be glued onto the back of the earring.

Develop a Strategy for Shopping:

• *Veteran flea-market shoppers develop a strategy for shopping. If you are looking for a particular item, attend preshow "early bird" openings. The higher admission price is a wise investment. If getting the best price is your main objective, shop the last few hours of the show. Vendors often lower their prices to avoid repacking or shipping the merchandise home.*

• *Work the show in an organized way so that you do not miss anything. Start at one end and go up one side and then down the other side of the aisle.*

When you have finished walking the entire show and you have the time, walk back through the show in the reverse order. You will be amazed what you see in a vendor's booth coming from the opposite direction.

• *You might want to do a quick walk through to see what is for sale. It is frustrating to buy a piece the first hour only to find the "perfect" piece three aisles over, or to find a very similar piece with a much cheaper price tag later on. The down side to this method is that when you return, the piece you wanted in the beginning may be sold.*

Petite Picture Frames

Earring Frame

Color-copy of photograph
Craft glue
Craft scissors
Epoxy
Vintage pearl clip earring

A jeweled clip earring may also be used, with the rhinestones glued on for framing the color-copy.

1 Remove the pearls from the ear-rings.

2 Crop the color-copy to the same dimensions as earring.

3 Using craft glue, glue the color-copy onto the earring front making certain that the bottom of picture is on the same end as clip hinge.

4 Using epoxy, glue the pearls around color-copy to frame picture.

5 Open the earring clip to create stand.

Rhinestone Frame

20-gauge wire
Cardboard
Color-copy of photograph
Craft glue
Craft scissors
Duct tape
Fabric scissors
Rhinestone brooch
Velvet fabric (scrap)
Wire cutters

1 Remove the center section and backing of the brooch to create frame opening. *Note: If a brooch is used that does not have an opening for photo placement, use wire cutters or metal shears to cut inside of the brooch, creating an opening.*

2 Cut a piece of cardboard to the same dimensions as brooch.

3 Crop the color-copy to the same dimensions as brooch.

4 Glue the color-copy onto the cardboard.

5 Cut the velvet to the same dimensions as brooch.

Beaded Belt-buckle Frame

20-gauge wire
Beaded belt buckle
Color-copy of photograph
Craft glue
Craft scissors
Duct tape
Fabric scissors
Velvet fabric (scrap)
Wire cutters

1 Remove the center section of the buckle to create frame opening.

2 Cut a piece of cardboard to the same dimensions as buckle.

3 Crop the color-copy to the same dimensions as buckle.

4 Glue the color-copy onto the cardboard.

5 Cut the velvet to the same dimensions as cardboard.

6 Cut the wire four times the length of frame. Shape the wire as shown in Diagram A to create a stand for frame.

7 Tape the wire ends of stand to the back side of cardboard.

8 Glue the velvet over the cardboard and wire ends of the stand as shown in the above photograph.

6 Cut wire four times the length of frame. Shape the wire as shown in Diagram A to create a stand for frame.

7 Tape the wire ends of stand to the back side of cardboard.

8 Glue the velvet over the cardboard and wire ends of the stand as shown in the above photograph.

9 (Optional) Additional rhinestones can be glued around edge if desired.

Diagram A

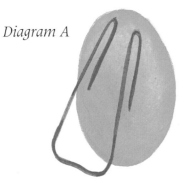

Crystal Drop Necklace

Chain necklaces (2)
Head pins
Needle-nosed pliers
Teardrop crystal beads (7)
Wire cutters

1 Place a head pin through each bead and cut off excess, leaving enough wire to form a loop at the top of bead.

2 Separate five graduated lengths of links from one necklace: one long, two midlength, and two short. Attach one end of each length to a looped end of a head pin.

3 Beginning with the center link of the second necklace, attach the top link of the longest drop bead. Repeat with the remaining lengths, graduating from longest to shortest on each side. Finish with the two remaining teardrop beads on the looped pin heads.

Trim Choker

Decorative fabric trim with globes
Fabric scissors
Jump rings
Needle-nosed pliers
Ringed faceted-crystal rhinestones
Small rhinestone-encrusted globes

Antique trims can be great sources for chokers, bracelets, and anklets. If you find a trim you like and the color is wrong, as was the case with this 1920s' trim which happened to be white, it can be dyed to a desired color. Any combination of old jewelry pieces can be combined and attached to embellish the trim.

1 Attach the jump rings to the jewelry pieces.

2 Cut the trim to desired length. Attach the jump rings through the cording on trim to hold the jewelry pieces in desired place.

3 Ends of choker are tied together when worn. *Note: Crimp beads and clasp fastener may be attached for a different type of closure.*

Jeweled Hair Accessories

Hair comb
Hairpins
Hot-glue gun
Jewelry findings (brooches, earrings)

1 Remove the backs from the earrings and pins.

2 Glue the jewelry findings onto the curved end of hairpins as desired.

3 Glue one jewelry setting onto the center of hair comb. Glue small, individual jewelry findings onto each side of center setting.

Once You Decide to Buy:

Don't hesitate—buy anything you can't live without on the spot. Chances are very good that you will not have another opportunity.

Don't head straight for the item you covet. Ask about several other items before negotiating for the one you really want.

Ask questions and look over the piece very carefully. You need not hurry. It may be damaged or a reproduction that you do not notice in the beginning.

Bargain, but do not be condescending, abrasive, or insulting with your offers. Simply ask: "Is this your best price?" or "What is the least amount you will take for this item?" If you buy several pieces from the same dealer they are more inclined to give you a discount.

Paying cash may also lead to a discount. Rain, unbearable heat, or a slow show can all work in the favor of the buyer in regards to pricing.

If you buy a major item that is expensive, always get full written documentation of age and value on a receipt. If the dealer refuses to put the information in writing, it may not be true.

Twisted-chain Necklace

Assorted silver jewelry
  baubles
Needle-nosed pliers
Red pebble beads
Twisted-chain necklace

1 Remove enough links from the necklace to use for jump rings and attach to the baubles and beads. *Note: Jump rings may be used if chain links cannot be removed.*

2 Attach the baubles and beads to necklace as desired.

What Are Collectibles?

The areas and periods now considered "collectible" are wider than ever before. In the fifties, anything made after the 1830s would not have been considered "antique" or "collectible." But in today's market, jewelry from the Art Nouveau and Art Deco periods are highly sought and command high prices.

Jewelry from the 1960s and 1970s has become quite popular and of more interest to collectors recently.

Costume jewelry, which was once thought of as junk and less than desirable, has become a longed-for collectible, with museum displays and books dedicated to the subject.

Pebble-beaded Necklace

Clasp fastener
Coin bracelet
Crimp beads (2)
Dangle earrings (2 pair)
Needle-nosed or crimping pliers
Red pebble beads
Silver and red glass bracelet
  (hinged links)
Tigertail wire
Wire cutters

1 Remove eight coins from the coin bracelet, leaving jump rings attached. Remove the jump ring from one edge of each coin and cut off loop. Set the removed jump rings aside for later use. *Note: Jump rings may be used if chain links cannot be removed.*

2 Remove the earring dangles, leaving jump rings attached.

3 Remove one bracelet link from the bracelet and attach a jump ring to one end. *Note: A hole may need to be drilled into one end of link to attach a jump ring.*

4 String the beads, dangles, and coins on the wire in the following sequence: eighteen beads and one coin three times, nine beads and one earring dangle, nine beads and one coin, nine beads and one earring dangle, nine beads and bracelet link. Continue stringing second half of necklace in reverse order.

5 Form a loop at one end of the wire and attach a crimp bead and one-half of clasp fastener. Repeat for remaining end.

Dressed-up Chandelier

Assorted beads
Beading wire
Chain
Crystal drops
Fabric glue
Jump rings
Ribbon
Vintage chandelier
Wire cutters

1 Drape the chain around and between the chandelier arms. Attach the chain with wire and jump rings where the chandelier crystals originally hung. *Note: Small holes may be drilled for attaching chain.*

2 Attach the beads and crystal drops to the chain and chandelier with wire as desired.

3 Glue the ribbon around the outside edges of light sockets.

Additional Flea Market Shopping Tips:

• *Dress for comfort, wear shoes that will hold up under any conditions.*

• *If going with friends, wear something that is brightly colored so that they can find you easily in a crowd.*

• *If you are going to be outside, wear layers so that if the temperature changes as the day progresses you can add or subtract sweaters and jackets.*

• *If there is any possibility of rain, take a waterproof poncho that folds up neatly and easily in a bag.*

• *Carry a large bag or a backpack, since vendors seldom have sturdy bags of their own. Make certain the bag can be tightly closed for the safekeeping of money, credit cards, and small purchased items.*

• *Be prepared to pay in cash. A lot of small purchases are difficult if they have to be charged or have checks written—and many dealers will take nothing but cash.*

Pillow Jewelry

Decorative pillow
Vintage brooch

A vintage brooch or a lone earring (with the back removed) may be attached to a pillow as well as short lengths of chain sewn to each corner for tassels.

1 Pin the brooch onto a decorative pillow to dress it up.

Chair Trim

Corded tassel
Sewing needle and thread
Upholstery pins
Vintage brooch

Upholstered furniture can be embellished with favorite pieces of jewelry that are large enough to make a statement.

1 Coil the tassel cord and stitch to secure. Attach the tassel to the chair where desired. Attach the brooch over the coil. *Note: Fabric glue or a hot-glue gun may be used to more permanently attach decorative elements.*

Jewelry Picture Hanger

Decorative tacks or nails
Epoxy
Framed picture
Hammer
Nail with large head
Vintage beaded or chain necklace
Vintage jewelry piece (brooch, earring, pendant)

Framed prints, photos, and paintings become more interesting when hung with vintage chain or bead necklaces.

1 Attach one end of the necklace to a top corner of frame with decorative tacks. Repeat for other side. *Note: Necklace may be attached to the back of the frame, if desired.*

2 Hammer the nail into the wall where picture will be hung. Glue the jewelry piece onto the head of nail to create a picture hook. Allow to dry thoroughly.

3 Hang the frame necklace over the hook to display picture.

Thimble Flower Brooches

Green Thimble Brooch

Beading wire
Epoxy
Florist tape
Green molding clay
Pin back
Pink flower buttons
Plastic thimble
Seed beads: blue, green, yellow
Tape measure
Wire cutters

1 Cut three 7" lengths of wire. String ten yellow beads onto one wire and slide beads to center. Bend the wire and twist two times below the beads to form a petal as shown in Diagram B.

2 String ten yellow beads onto one end of wire. Bend the wire and twist as in Step 1 to form a second petal. Repeat on opposite side of wire. Alternate sides, stringing beads onto the wire until five petals have been formed.

3 Bend and shape the petals as desired. Bring the short end of wire up through the center and string on two blue beads to form the center of flower. Bend the wire up and over the flower center and back down. Twist the wires together to secure and form stem. Repeat Steps 1–3 for remaining flowers.

4 Cut five 3" lengths of wire. String fifteen beads onto one wire and slide beads to

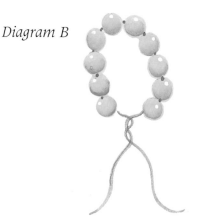

Diagram B

center. Bend and shape the wire to form a leaf. Twist the wires together to secure and form stem. Repeat for remaining leaves. *Note: Smaller leaves may be made by stringing on a lesser number of beads.*

5 Cut two 6" lengths of wire. String a button onto one wire and slide button to center. Bend the wire and twist two times below the button to secure and form stem. Repeat for remaining buttons.

6 Wrap the wire stems of flowers and leaves with floral tape.

7 Place a small amount of molding clay into the thimble. Insert the flowers and leaves into the clay and arrange as desired.

8 Glue the pin back onto the side of thimble.

Beading wire
Epoxy
Florist tape
Green molding clay
Pin back
Pink flower buttons
Plastic thimble
Seed beads: green, yellow
Tape measure
Wire cutters

A metal thimble may be painted and used in place of a plastic thimble.

1 Cut three 3" lengths of wire. String five yellow beads onto one wire and slide beads to center. Bend the wire and twist two times below the beads to form a tiny flower as shown in Diagram B on page 34. Repeat for remaining flowers.

2 Cut four 3" lengths of wire. String fifteen green beads onto one wire and slide beads to center. Bend the wire and twist two times below the beads to form a leaf. Repeat for remaining leaves. *Note: Smaller leaves may be made by stringing on a lesser number of beads.*

3 Cut three 6" lengths of wire. String the button onto one wire and slide button to

center. Bend the wire and twist two times below the button to secure and form stem. Repeat for remaining buttons.

4 Wrap the wire stems of flowers and leaves with floral tape.

5 Place a small amount of molding clay into the thimble. Insert the flowers and leaves into the clay and arrange as desired.

6 Glue the pin back onto the side of thimble.

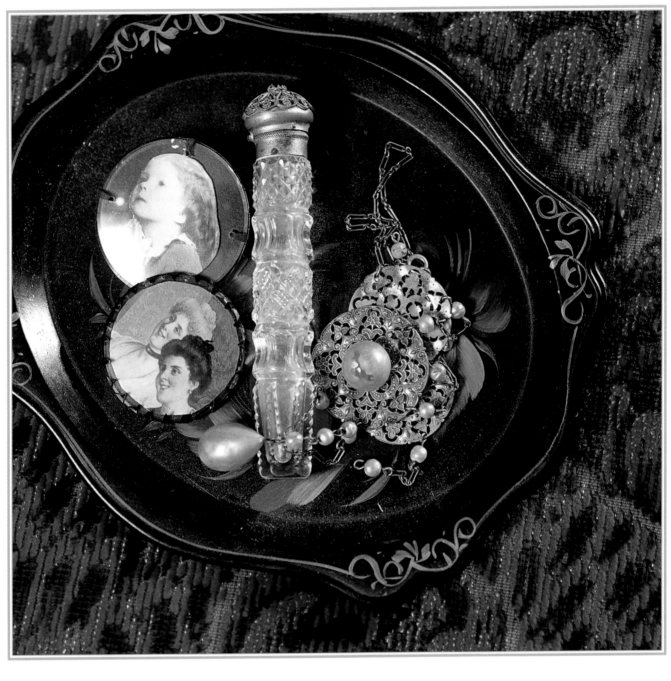

Pocket Watch Photo Brooches

Pronged–setting Photo Brooch

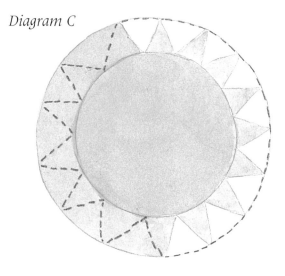

Diagram C

Aluminum or other lightweight metal
    sheeting
Black permanent marker
Color-copy of photograph
Craft scissors
Epoxy
Needle-nosed pliers
Pin back
Pocket or large watch crystal
Ruler
Wire cutters or metal shears

This crystal was removed from a pocket watch, but any large-faced crystal could be used. A pronged setting from vintage costume jewelry could also be used for this brooch.

1   Crop the color-copy to the same dimensions as crystal.

2   Cut a circle from the aluminum sheeting ⅜" larger than the crystal. Cut ⅜" triangles from the edge of circle as shown in Diagram C to create pronged setting.

3   Color the back side of prongs and the edge of circle black.

4   Place the color-copy behind the crystal and center the crystal on the setting. Bend the prongs over the crystal to secure.

5   Glue the pin back onto the back side of setting.

Photo Watch Crystal Brooch

Card stock
Color-copy of photograph
Craft scissors
Epoxy
Pin back
Pocket or large watch crystal (with drilled holes)
Sewing needle and thread

1 Crop the color-copy to the same dimensions as crystal.

2 Cut the card stock to the same dimensions as crystal.

3 Place the color-copy behind the crystal and the card stock behind the color-copy.

4 Attach the color-copy and card stock to the watch crystal by stitching through the holes in crystal and around the edge. Knot to secure.

5 Glue the pin back onto the card stock.

Popular Stones and Materials of the 1920s and 1930s:

• *Emeralds were cut into a square or rectangle, which was well suited to Art Deco design elements.*

• *Rubies, both genuine and synthetic, were desirable because of their bold red color which created a dramatic effect.*

• *Marcasites, cut from pyrite, were fashionable replacements for diamonds. They were typically set in silver as were the diamonds of these periods.*

• *Ivory became popular with a renewed cultural interest in African carvings. Ivory from the hippopotamus and walrus were used as well as the elephant. Vegetable ivories, from the coroze nut and the doum-palm nut were also used for making beads and small jewelry items and are often mistaken for real ivory.*

• *Bakelite®, a plastic resin that can be molded or cast, was developed and became quite popular for use in jewelry items.*

• *Pearls were in demand for necklaces and with the refinement of the cultured pearl, they were affordable to the average person.*

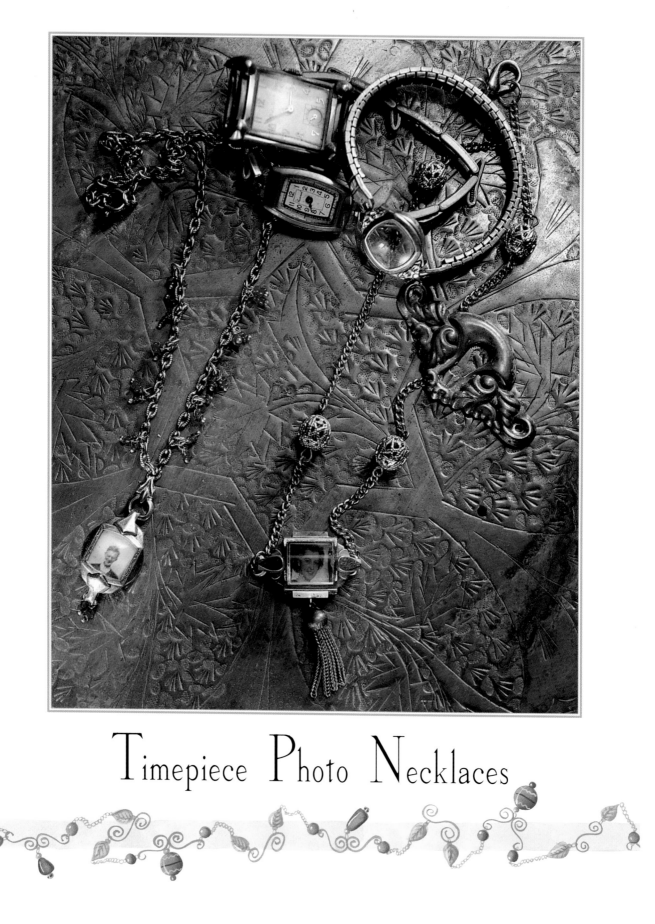

Timepiece Photo Necklaces

Pendant Timepiece Photo Necklace

Chain or link necklace
Color-copy of photograph
Head pins
Needle-nosed pliers
Seed beads
Small jump rings
Vintage wristwatch (with
    linked band)

1 Remove the band from the wristwatch. Open the watch case and remove the crystal and internal workings.

2 Crop the color-copy to the same dimensions as crystal. Place the color-copy behind the crystal. Replace the crystal with color-copy inside the case and close.

3 Attach a jump ring to the top side of case.

4 Attach the case jump ring to the center link of necklace.

5 String seed beads onto head pins as desired and cut off excess, leaving enough wire to form a loop at the top of beads.

6 Attach head pins to chain necklace and bottom side of case with jump rings.

Tasseled Timepiece Photo Necklace

Chain necklace (with metal
    beads)
Chain tassel
Color-copy of photograph
Jump rings
Needle-nosed pliers
Vintage wristwatch (with
    linked band)
Wire cutters

1 Remove the band from the wristwatch. Open the watch case and remove the crystal and internal workings.

2 Crop the color-copy to the same dimensions as crystal. Place the color-copy behind the crystal. Replace the crystal with color-copy inside the case and close.

3 Attach the jump rings to each side of case.

4 Separate the two center links of the necklace and attach each link to jump rings.

5 Attach the tassel to the stem side of case with jump rings.

Key Collection
Necklace

Bead and chain necklace
Jump rings
Needle-nosed pliers
Vintage keys

Display a collection of antique keys on an attractive vintage necklace around the neck or to decorate a vintage lamp shade.

1 Separate several lengths of beads and links from the necklace to create drops.

2 Attach a key to one drop with a jump ring. Repeat for remaining keys and drops.

3 Attach key drops to necklace with jump rings as desired.

Faux Pearl Bracelet

Beading wire
Chain bracelet
Faux pearls
Large seed beads
Needle-nosed pliers
Tape measure
Wire cutters

Creamy faux pearls and seed beads were used to adorn this chain bracelet. Any type or combination of beads may be used to give a new look to a plain bracelet.

1 Determine the number of beads and pearls to attach to the bracelet and cut one 2" piece of wire for each pearl. *Note: The pearls were placed on every other link in the bracelet shown.*

2 Thread the end of one wire through a pearl and a seed bead, then back through the pearl as shown in above photograph. Twist wire ends together to secure. Repeat for remaining pearls.

3 Attach the beaded pearl to a bracelet link by threading one end of wire through link and twisting to secure. Cut off excess wire.

Tigereye Necklace

18-gauge sterling silver wire
Clasp fastener
Crimp beads (2)
Jump rings
Needle-nosed or crimping pliers
Oval and round stone beads
Round-nosed jewelry pliers
Tigereye beads
Tigereye stones (3)
Tigertail wire
Wire cutters

1 Cut one length of sterling silver wire to wrap around one tigereye stone, leaving 1" at top and bottom. Wrap the wire around the stone and form into a spiral at bottom.

2 Form the wire at top into a loop, leaving a tail. Wrap the tail around the wire loop at top of stone to secure.

3 Repeat Steps 1 and 2 for the remaining tigereye stones.

4 String one stone onto the tigertail wire and slide to center. Place three tigereye beads on each side of stone. String one stone onto each side of beads.

5 String the remaining beads onto the wire in desired sequence.

6 Form a loop at one end of wire and attach a crimp bead and one-half of clasp fastener. Repeat for the remaining end.

Seashell Brooch

14-gauge brass wire
Bell caps
Bracelet with leaf links
Cowrie seashell necklace
Epoxy
Metal filigree candleholder
   (See page 46)
Metal shears
Needle-nosed pliers
Pin back
Wire cutters

1 Cut one leaf shape from the filigree for the brooch base and flatten if necessary.

2 Separate the bracelet leaf links and remove the jump rings as necessary. *Note: Leaf shapes may be cut from sheet metal.*

3 Place and glue leaf links onto the filigree as desired.

4 Cut and curl one end of wire length for a leaf stem. Glue the stem onto the center of filigree.

5 Remove the shells from the necklace. Attach the bell caps to the small end of shells.

6 Glue the flat side of one shell onto each leaf link.

7 Glue the pin back onto the back side of filigree.

Beads & Baubles Necklace

Bead and chain necklace
Beading wire
Crystal drop
Epoxy
Metal filigree candleholder
Metal shears
Needle-nosed pliers
Wire cutters

A metal filigree candleholder serves many purposes when making jewelry with flea-market finds. A simple bead and chain necklace becomes more significant when filigree and a drop crystal are added to it.

Crimson Drop Earrings

Assorted beads
French ear wires (2)
Needle-nosed pliers
Pin heads (2)
Wire cutters

An assortment of vintage beads were used to make these drop earrings.

1 String beads onto a head pin as desired and cut off excess, leaving enough wire to form a loop at the top of the bead. Repeat for the remaining head pin.

2 Attach one ear wire to a looped end of a head pin.

1 Cut two mirror-
image pieces from
the filigree design.

2 Shape the pieces into
a slightly convex
form. Glue the pieces
with wrong sides
together to create
amulet.

3 Separate the two
center links of neck-
lace. Form two jump
rings from the wire and
attach the upper edges
of amulet to the neck-
lace links.

4 Form a jump ring
from the wire and
attach the crystal drop
to the bottom of
amulet.

Photo Brooches

Card stock
Color-copy of photograph
Craft scissors
Decoupage medium
Vintage Brooch

Antique pins that are missing jewels need not be discarded. These will make beautiful photo pins.

1 Remove desired jewel from the brooch setting to create frame.

2 Crop the color-copy to the same dimensions as setting.

3 Cut the card stock to the same dimensions as setting.

4 Glue the color-copy onto the card stock. Glue the color-copy into the setting.

5 Pour decoupage medium over the color-copy for a thick, smooth coat and allow to dry.

Watchband Bracelet

Beading wire
Epoxy
Men's watchband (stretch type)
Needle-nosed pliers
Rhinestone earring
Wire cutters

A man's watchband is large and provides the extra room that would be lacking in a lady's watchband when the face is removed. A brooch or pendant could be substituted for the earring.

1 Wire the watchband ends together to create bracelet.

2 Remove the earring back and glue the earring onto the center of bracelet.

Filigree Cuff Bracelet

Epoxy
Metal file
Metal filigree candleholder
Metal shears
Needle-nosed pliers
Tape measure
Vintage earring

A lone earring adds a decorative touch to this metal filigree cuff bracelet.

1 Measure the wrist and add ½" for the band measurement. Cut one strip 1"–1¼" by band measurement from the filigree candleholder to create bracelet. *Note: This candleholder had a natural band design around it.*

2 File the bracelet edges smooth and bend the ends of the bracelet under ¼". Shape the bracelet to fit the wrist.

3 Remove the earring back and glue the earring onto the center of bracelet.

Gypsy Princess Crowns

Beading wire
Epoxy
Jewelry findings (beads, brooches,
    earrings, jewels)
Metal file
Metal filigree or band
Metal shears
Needle-nosed pliers
Tape measure
Wire cutters

*The metal used for the bands in these crowns came
from vintage glass soap dishes that had metal-
trimmed bottoms.*

1 Cut the crown band to the desired length
and width. File edges smooth where necessary. Bend inside edges under ¼".

2 Remove the earring and brooch backs. Wire
and/or glue the jewelry findings onto the
crown as desired.

Jewelry Trends of the 1940s:

• *Retro Modern, Victorian-inspired designs, costume jewelry, and over-sized earrings and rings replaced the sleek and streamlined geometric designs of the Art Deco influence of the 1920s and 1930s.*

• *Small hair combs with 14-karat gold tops, gold barrettes, and gold hairpins with screw-on gold snowflakes were popular trims for women's hair.*

• *Sterling bicycle clips were a popular accessory and used for holding up sweater sleeves and clipping in slack legs.*

• *Sunbursts and dome-shaped earrings and bracelets were popular with the average woman and were imitations of more costly jewelry.*

• *The Victorian scroll motifs and flower sprays, along with the return of white metal finishes, describe this decade.*

51

Pearl Headpiece

Crimp beads (4)
Jump ring
Long string of pearls
Needle-nosed pliers
Pearl drop earring or pendant
Tape measure
Tigertail wire
Wire cutters

1 Measure the circumference of the head plus 2". Cut a length of tigertail to that measurement.

2 String the pearls onto the tigertail. Form a loop at each end of the tigertail and secure with a crimp bead.

3 Measure from the top of the forehead to just past the crown plus 2". Cut a length of tigertail to that measurement.

4 Form a loop at one end of tigertail and secure with a crimp bead. String the pearls onto the tigertail.

5 Loop uncrimped end of tigertail over the center of first length of pearls and secure with a crimp bead.

6 Remove the pearl drop from the earring back. Bring the three looped ends of pearls together and attach to the pearl drop with a jump ring.

Ring Bracelet

Bead and chain necklace
Beading wire
Brass band bracelet
Brass locket
Brass ring
Color-copy of photograph
Drill with small drill bits
Epoxy
Needle-nosed pliers
Tape measure
Wire cutters

1 Center and drill two holes 2" apart on one edge of bracelet.

2 Remove any decoration from the ring. Glue the locket onto the top of ring.

3 Place the bracelet on the wrist and the ring on a finger. Measure the distance from the ring to one drilled hole. Separate a length of necklace just slightly longer than that measurement. Repeat for remaining drilled hole.

4 Attach the first necklace length to the bracelet hole with wire. Repeat for the remaining necklace length.

5 Attach both necklace lengths to the ring with wire. *Note: Jump rings may be used in place of wire.*

6 Crop color-copy to the locket dimensions. Place the color-copy inside of locket.

Beaded Curtain

18-gauge wire
Assorted beads
Jewelry findings
Needle-nosed pliers
Tape measure
Wire cutters

1 Cut the wire into 3"–4" lengths.

2 String the bead(s) and/or jewelry findings onto a length of wire.

3 Form coils or swirls to attach the lengths together as shown in close-up photograph below. Make the linked strands to desired length.

4 Attach multiple strands to windows, doorways, or other openings as desired.

Beaded Wind Chime

Assorted beads (metal, pony, wooden, etc.)
Brass ceiling-mount lamp fixture
Craft scissors
Drill and small drill bits
Hemp string (thin)
Large-eye needle
Metal jewelry findings (drops from earrings and necklaces)
Paper beads (See instructions at right)
Tape measure

1 Drill holes approximately 1" apart around the outside edge of lamp fixture.

2 Drill three evenly spaced holes around the top edge of lamp fixture for attaching the hanger.

3 Cut one varying length of string for each outside-edge hole.

4 Tie a jewelry finding onto the end of one length. Repeat for the remaining lengths.

5 String the beads onto each length as desired. Thread through hole and knot the strand of beads onto the lamp fixture. Repeat for the remaining lengths.

6 Cut three equal lengths from string. Thread the end of one length through one hole at top of fixture and knot. Repeat for the remaining lengths. Pull the three lengths together and knot.

Paper Beads

Acrylic sealer
Craft glue
Craft scissors
Patterned papers
Small crochet hook
Small paintbrush

1 Cut the paper into long rectangles. *Note: The height and length of the rectangle will determine the length and diameter of the finished bead.*

2 Cut the rectangles in half diagonally as shown in Diagram D.

3 Apply a thin layer of glue to the back side of the narrow two-thirds of one triangle. Beginning with the wide end, wrap the triangle around the crochet hook to create a bead. Remove and allow to dry thoroughly. Repeat for the remaining triangles.

4 Brush sealer over the outside of the beads and allow to dry.

Diagram D

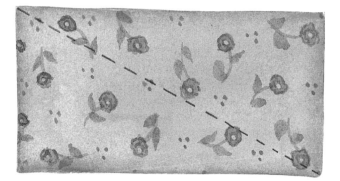

Embellished Bags

Beaded-trim Bag

Assorted beads
Bag (handmade or purchased)
Beaded trim
Beading thread
Fabric scissors
Jewelry finding (brooch, buckle,
  earring, etc.)
Sewing needle and thread
Thin cording

This bag was made from vintage fabric and adorned with beads.

1 Stitch the beaded trim around the bottom of bag.

2 String the beads onto desired lengths of beading thread for fringe. Stitch each beaded length to the bottom edge of bag.

3 String the beads onto the cording to create handle. Stitch the handle onto the bag.

4 Attach the jewelry finding to the bag flap as desired.

Butterfly-trimmed Bag

Bag (handmade or purchased)
Brooch

1 Pin the brooch to one side of bag to dress it up.

Jewelry Trends of the 1950s:

• Costume jewelry remains popular, with earrings as large as silver dollars, large pearl buttons, and floral bouquet motifs.

• The advent of the chemise and its simplicity of design called for costume jewelry in the form of multiple strands of beads, bracelets, and earrings that hung from the earlobe to the shoulder.

• Jewelry made from resin such as Bakelite® continues to be popular with the masses.

Darcia Dudman

Darcia was born in Ogden, Utah, on April Fool's Day 1967. She calls it "In the Spring before the Summer of Love." She currently lives in Salt Lake City, Utah, with Chase, her beautiful Dalmatian.

As a child, she spent many happy hours at her grandmother's house. Her favorite toy? Grandmother's jewelry box, of course! She has a beautiful collection of rhinestone, crystal, and gemstone pieces. Darcia would sit for hours, fascinated with the colorful, sparkling jewels spread out across grandmother's bed. Her grandmother had pieces that had belonged to her mother from the twenties and thirties, and her own cocktail-style jewelry from the forties, fifties, and sixties, as well as beautiful silver and beads from her extensive travels.

Because of her grandmother, Darcia will always be drawn to vintage jewelry. She was a child through the turbulent seventies, in junior high during the Disco era, in high school with the neon new wave, and the punk and MTV influence of the 1980s, which was followed by the hip hop culture in college. She later survived the grunge fad that gave way to the more austere fashions of the nineties. She has learned, firsthand, that extremes in fashion come and go, but classic, vintage styles will always be appreciated.

She graduated from the University of Utah in 1990 with a B.A. in English. Following graduation, she traveled and held a variety of sales jobs. She sold everything—clothing, home furnishings, African art, fine art, and of course, jewelry. She briefly attended the Gemological Institute of America and a private design school in New York City— Studio Jewelers LTD.

In 1995, Darcia, along with some close friends, opened **Black & White**, a jewelry and gift shop in Provo, Utah, which she has since moved to Salt Lake City, Utah. Once the store was up and running, Darcia began designing and selling her own line of jewelry. She believes that jewelry can be worn comfortably and enjoyed.

The fashion trend since the 1990s has been very minimalist and her biggest design challenge has been to integrate the ornate vintage jewelry components with the clean current contemporary styles. She combines the old and new to create wearable modern designs with a vintage twist.

Darcia loves the decadent opulence of vintage jewelry as well as the more practical understated new styles. She believes that the mix of the old and new, past and present, bare minimalist and high-impact ornate is truly the style of today.

Upper, left to right: This necklace is made from a triple strand of vintage glass beads trimmed with a costume accent. ▦ Blue glass seed beads, Austrian crystal, and a drop made from a faux pearl and brass chain adorn this necklace. ▦ Oxidized metal wire, vintage faux pearls, and Czech crystals are the components that make up this necklace.

Lower, left to right: This necklace is created from vintage and faceted-crystal beads, knotted with black polyester string. ▦ A vintage button is strung along with faceted smoky quartz beads and freshwater pearls to make this necklace.

Upper, left to right: This necklace consists of a knotted strand of Czech crystal, with a doubled strand of tanzanite and a vintage drop from an earring. ▣ A flea-market brass chain, a knotted strand of pink tourmaline, and a vintage earring centerpiece are the components in this necklace. ▣ This necklace is created from Montana blue swarovski crystal, and aurora borealis white beads with an antique rhinestone accent.

Lower, left to right: This necklace is strung with Czech and Austrian crystal beads and embellished with a costume jewelry earring. ▣ Aquamarine beads on a knotted strand, doubled with a tiny garnet strand and a vintage earring centerpiece make up the necklace.

Jody Lyons

Clockwise: The centerpiece for this brooch is a resin piece from China with semiprecious stones and Bakelite® beads. ▣ Brooch consists of a jade shoe carving, 1950s' and 1960s' plastic pieces and beads, along with 1950s' and 1960s' glass beads. ▣ Bakelite® faces and 1930s' and 1960s' glass are used in this brooch and barrette. ▣ A barrette that is made from 1950s' and 1960s' plastics and 1930s' glass.

Jody Lyons started **Joli Jewelry** in 1984 after having her personal jewelry stolen while she was in college. After not being able to find jewelry that she liked in neighboring shops at prices she could afford, she began making jewelry by collecting vintages pieces and parts that include deco glass; Bakelite®, celluloid, and other vintage plastics; old French enamels; and mother-of-pearl buttons. She combines these with semiprecious stones and other types of new and old components. Each piece is handmade and a limited edition, often inspired by the Moderne and Art Deco periods, as well as by the colors, textures, and shapes of unusual findings.

Clockwise: Brooch composed of semiprecious stones and Bakelite® plastics on a black onyx base. ▣ *Bakelite® vases, 1950s' and 1960s' plastics, and semiprecious stones are used to create these brooches.* ▣ *This brooch is made from Bakelite® pieces.* ▣ *A hat pin top, Carnival glass, and 1920s' glass.* ▣ *A hat pin top, 1920s' glass around the edge, and pyrite beads embellish this barrette.* ▣ *This brooch is designed using 1920s'–1930s' milk glass and Art Deco glass pieces.*

The two hair combs and the upper right brooch are made from Bakelite® and celluloid. ▩ The brooch at bottom right is constructed from Bakelite®, coral beads, and a 1950s' glass dragon button.

Upper: The upper left pair of earrings are made from 1920s' and 1930s' glass. ▨ *The remaining two pairs of earrings contain coral beads, 1930s' and 1950s' glass, and Chinese turquoise.* ▨ *The brooch at lower right is embellished with 1950s' enamel and Bakelite® game chips.*

Right, clockwise: A bowling sport stone from the 1950s' and lucite from the 1960s' are primary design elements in this brooch. ▨ *Drop earrings are created using 1930s' and 1960s' glass as well as new glass.* ▨ *A base of frosted crystal is adorned with 1920s' and 1930s' glass.* ▨ *Earrings are made from 1920s' glass with new crystal drops.* ▨ *A dog sport stone, 1960s' and 1970s' Bakelite®, and newer plastic make up this brooch.* ▨ *Daisy earrings are made 1940s' glass and 1950s' plastic, including Bakelite®.*

Matching barrette, earrings, and brooch are made from 1920s' and 1930s' glass with onyx drops on the earrings and brooch. The brooch is also accented with lapis lazuli. ▦ Brooch at left contains 1940s'–1960s' glass, 1960s' plastic coral beads, and a knotted portion of a 1950s' Italian beaded necklace.

Clockwise, beginning with far right: This brooch contains serpentine jade and 1960s' plastic beads. ▣ 1930s' beads on a celluloid base adorn this brooch. ▣ The amber brooch at the far left contains an intaglio of the three graces—faith, hope, and charity—from the 1940s. ▣ The remaining jewelry pieces contain jewelry elements of 1930s' and 1950s' glass and findings from the Art Deco period.

Rhonda Kuhlman & Chris Ake

Recycled Works of Art is the creative partnership of Rhonda Kuhlman and Chris Ake. Together, they design and hand-produce a line of unique and functional jewelry, home accessories, and whimsical art pieces—all with a folk-art flair.

In 1992, they found themselves out of art school and in the real world, with a true desire to do something creative as a team. They determined to turn their obsessive collecting into fun pieces of folk art. At the heart of every piece they design is a bottle cap and their accumulated collection of over a million bottle caps has become their line of bottle-cap jewelry. The vintage bottle caps, from the 1930s to the 1970s, give their work that nostalgic Americana feel. Their love for pop culture naturally led them into combining their favorite images and religious icons with their art.

Their mix of funky Americana shows through in Chris's tinwork of Christmas ornaments, refrigerator magnets, and the more elaborate mirrors, retablos, and wall sculptures—all one of a kind. Every piece of tin is hand-cut and hand-tooled from recycled olive oil cans, soda pop cans, and roofing tin. Chris's style of tinwork maintains a respect for the legacy of tinwork from Mexico. However, his modern use of materials and detailed tooling give it the flair that has become uniquely his style.

Their desire to recycle is as obsessive as their collecting. They work with a number of different recycled items ranging from tin cans and soda pop cans to game pieces and records. Rhonda has had rubber molds made from the old plastic charms that were prizes in Crackerjack® boxes, and Barbie® purses and shoes. These are then hand-casted in silver to be used as accents.

As working artists, Rhonda and Chris have exhibited work with a more personal flair in numerous juried shows. **Recycled Works of Art** products have been exhibited in the United States and internationally. Their work can be found in a number of museum shops, galleries, and retail stores. Chris is the author of *Crafting with Metal* which features his tinwork.

A vintage 1978 record and colorful bottle caps have been recycled into a wall clock.

This cowgirls collector's necklace is made from recycled bottle caps and hand-casted charms. The laminated cowgirl faces are from vintage comics.

Opposite page, upper right: The bottle-cap choker and matching bracelet are made from vintage bottle caps that are hand-punched and linked together.

Opposite page, upper left: A recycled angel is made from vintage bottle caps that are hand-cut and punched. Hand-casted silver charms accent the bottle caps.

Opposite page, lower: These miniature bottle-cap chairs are the perfect accent pieces for a table made from a vintage milk cap. The wire used on the table and chairs is recycled from champagne bottles.

Right: This "glamour girl" choker is made from recycled bottle caps and laminated images. These images are cropped from collector cards packaged in 1930s' cigarettes.

Recycled juice cans, marbles, and dice are used to display a collection of bottle-cap earrings. The earrings are made from bottle caps and embellished with resin, glitter, and vintage images.

Debra Dresler

Debra Dresler, a Minnesota designer, has always been an antique and flea-market scrounger as well as a collector of "interesting-looking little things."

Her "view of art" comes from the beauty of everyday things. She reminds people to take a second look at that which they take for granted. She has always loved the tokens and pieces to children's games, antique typewriter keys, beach pebbles, coins, and anything industrial from the surplus stores. She uses these nontraditional materials to produce everyday useful objects like watches and clocks. She hopes to surprise people and give them a new perspective at the way we divide and measure out our days—that thing we call TIME.

Debra studied art and art history at the University of Wisconsin and has been an artist for over twenty years. Before pursuing her jewelry business, she worked as a photographer and a calligrapher, as well as a designer of fabrics and interior wall coverings.

"Cash Register" Cuff Bracelet
This bracelet is made from vintage cash register money plates and sterling silver.

Photo credit: Robert Diamante

Upper: "Cash Register" Bracelet
Buttons and parts from an antique cash
register and brass components make up
this bracelet.

Lower: "Balance Your Time" Watch
This quartz, battery-operated watch is
made from liquid-filled construction
level pieces.

Photo credits: Robert Diamante

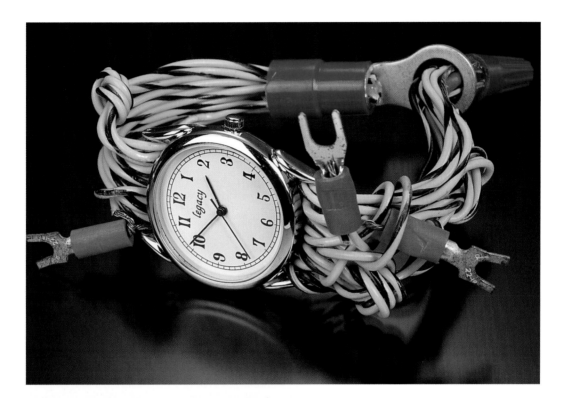

Upper: "Wired" Watch
Electrical components and wire make up the band on this quartz, battery-operated watch.

Lower: "Out of Time" Watch
This quartz, battery-operated watch is created from discarded parking meter parts and sterling silver.

Photo credits: Robert Diamante

Mary Jo Hiney

family, and the joy of life. Her lifelong love of ribbon inspired her to develop many of her own techniques, many of which are displayed in her gallery.

Mary Jo works as a freelance author and designer in the fabric and craft industry, gladly sharing secrets gathered in a lifetime of experience. She is the prolific author of *The Beaded Object, Fabulous Fabrics, Beautiful Foundation-Pieced Quilt Blocks, Creating with Lace, Decorative Fabric Covered Boxes, Ribbon Basics, Romantic Fabric-Covered Boxes, Romantic Silk Ribbon Keepsakes, Two-Hour Vests,* and *Victorian Ribbon and Lacecraft Designs.*

Mary Jo Hiney has avidly and continuously worked in craft and fabric-related fields for the past twenty-five years, and hopes to continue for the next twenty-four years! Her focus is on gifts and decorative accessories, her one-of-a-kind pieces display beauty always enhanced with function.

She attended the Fashion Institute of Design and Merchandising in Los Angeles, California. She worked in the downtown garment industry before moving on to NBC in Burbank, California, where she worked in the wardrobe department, dressing a diverse group of stars. She and her family later moved to the beautiful and tranquil central coast of California. It is here that Mary Jo discovered her creative genius, the love of raising a

A flea-market rhinestone brooch is pinned onto a favored hat for an added accent.

A lace-covered hatbox is further embellished with ribbon, lace, rhinestone dangle earrings, and a necklace locket. Bracelet charms and vintage buttons are also used for accents.

A collectible Victorian Valentine card is placed in a lace and fabric-covered frame. Ribbon embroidery and flowers, a vintage watch face, charms, lockets, rhinestones, assorted beads and buttons, and a rhinestone brooch add the final decorative Victorian touch.

Upper: A decorative and dainty wedding garter is accented with a rhinestone necklace pendant, charms, assorted beads, and ribbon flowers.

Right: Vintage jewelry findings, including teardrop pearls and faceted-crystal beads, are reassembled to create this beautiful necklace.

A heart-shaped box is covered with vintage fabric and embellished with bracelet charms, beads, buttons, lace, and ribbon.

Upper left: The focal point of this darling handmade, fabric-covered heart box is a rhinestone brooch.

Lower left: A brass earring, charm, rhinestone earring, and assorted antique buttons are added to beautify this fabric-covered box with metallic trim.

Upper right: A ribbon brooch is accented with buttons and jewelry findings from antique earrings and brooches.

Jo Packham & Chapelle Designers

Jo was born in Ogden, Utah, to the parents to whom she owes her dreams. All of their, and her life, they have been honest, good people who worked hard and taught their two daughters to be and do the same. Jo's mother, who is wiser than her educated years, made her believe that there wasn't anything she could not accomplish—she simply needed to learn how. And not only could Jo accomplish it, but she could do it with a champagne appetite (which she inherited from her father) on a beer budget. She is certain it all began when her mother made her own prom dress from the living-room curtains—and through all of Jo's school years, her mother created the same magic for her.

Jo graduated with honors in Art from the University of California at Sacramento. Upon graduation, she returned home and opened Apple Arts, a retail store that sold art supplies. She decided the retail industry wasn't for her and started The Vanessa-Ann Collection with very little money, a good idea, and an uncontrollable passion.

All of her life Jo has admired and loved the work made by artisans, and wanted to work with these yet unknown friends and surround herself with every aspect of what they so love to do.

Since the beginning, Chapelle has worked with the most respected and accomplished artisans in their fields, producing books ranging from home decorating and gardening to master woodworking and antique needle arts.

That was twenty-two years ago, in which time she was blessed with a son, a daughter, and a son-in-law, whom she adores more than words can describe. Jo has been honored with YWCA's first "Business of the Year" Award, has received numerous awards within her industry for prize-winning photography, and has traveled around the country teaching and consulting. She has authored thirteen of her own publications and is responsible for the publication of approximately 200 titles, which have been designed and written by over 100 individual authors.

Jo lives in Ogden in a home that was built in 1929, which she is renovating with her husband. They live there with his garden and his aquarium, her daughter's five cats, and her son's dog.

She has been blessed with both the "best of times and the worst of times," which she believes is needed to make one understand and appreciate all that life has to offer.

Jewelry tree: This small tree is decorated with necklaces, pendants, earrings, and other jewelry findings.

Jewelry tree detail: Vintage jewelry adornments.

Formal dress tree (opposite page): A vintage evening gown on a flea-market sewing form is further embellished with antique jewelry findings.

Waist detail (upper): Costume jewelry is on display in this close-up detail of the evening gown.

Dress detail (right): A rhinestone necklace and other antique costume jewelry findings finish off the look.

*Welcome to Wonderland: Assorted beads, taken from old necklaces,
are strung onto jewelry wire, and nineteen 1" round metal-edged
tags with silver lettering, spelling out "Welcome to Wonderland,"
are evenly spaced between the beads.*

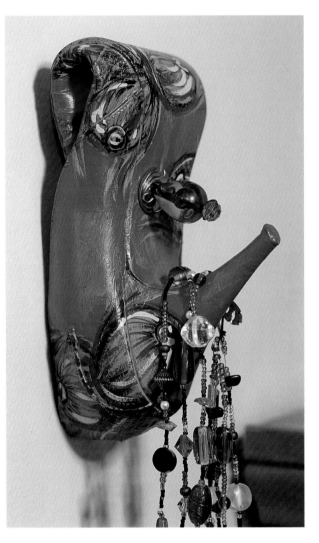

Hookers (left): Hand-painted "Hookers" (heels) are attached to the wall and used to hold assorted beaded necklaces. (Hookers are made, using vintage shoes and jewelry-adorned hangers to hold them in place, by Studio Normand in Tularosa, New Mexico.)

Hookers detail (upper): A jeweled nail is used to attach the heel to the wall.

Hanging frames: For a unique and uncommon decorative element, drawer pulls are hung on the wall as picture hooks, and long necklaces are used to hang these ornate, carved picture frames.

Hanging frames detail (opposite page): Necklaces are draped and wrapped around frames.

Curtain embellishments (upper): Beaded grapes found at a jewelry store are used as a decorative element on curtains. (Curtain embellishments designed and created by Susan Ure.)

Chair accents (right): A beaded tassel is hung over an enameled urn. The miniature Japanese urns are glued on the top of the chair as finials.

Antiques and trinkets quilt: This handmade quilt is pieced from cotton muslin and quilted. The quilt is embellished with an antique mother-of-pearl pin that says "Mother," embroidery, crocheted trim, doilies, antique buttons, and assorted, faceted-crystal and pearl beads. (Quilt designed and made by Susan Whitelock.)

Satin button wreath: A small stuffed satin wreath is embellished with white and crystal buttons that were taken from old garments, then hung with gold cording.

Beaded chandelier: Monofilament fiber is strung with assorted vintage and new beads into several long strands. Long necklaces could also be used. The beaded strands are draped around and attached to the chandelier. (Beaded chandelier is created by Susan Ure.)

Brooch napkin fasteners: Brooches are pinned to napkins in place of napkin rings.

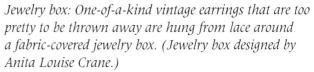

Jewelry box: One-of-a-kind vintage earrings that are too pretty to be thrown away are hung from lace around a fabric-covered jewelry box. (Jewelry box designed by Anita Louise Crane.)

Pearl-draped vase: A flea-market strand of faux pearls are looped and draped around the neck of a simple vase as an added accent. (Vase designed by Jill Williams Grover.)

*Framed brooch: A cherished antique brooch is placed in
a hand-painted frame and used as a décor accent.*

Button wreath: Brass jewelry and buttons are strung onto beading wire and wrapped around a 3" brass ring. Wired-edged ribbon is tied onto the wreath as a decorative element and for hanging.

Link and button bracelet: The shanks are removed from assorted metal buttons, and the buttons are then glued onto the flat connectors of a flea-market link bracelet.

Button and jeweled-mesh bracelet: Assorted buttons, brooches, and earrings are stitched onto a ¼" metallic elastic ribbon with nylon thread. A buttonhole and button are used for a closure.

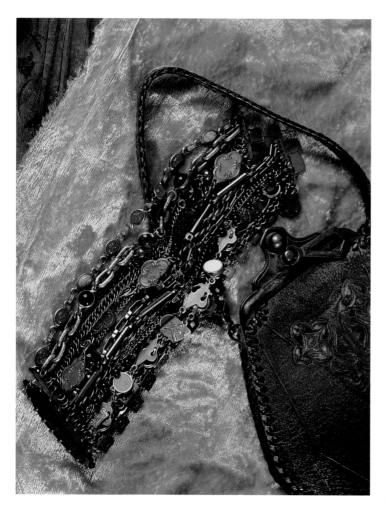

Multistrand bracelet: A variety of flea-market bracelets and chains are attached to a 2"-long bead in cup with multiple loops. The remaining ends of the bracelets and chains are attached to a 1" and a ¾" multistrand clasp.

Beaded button ring: This ring is made from a burnished metallic antique button and delica seed beads strung on a stretchy monofilament beading elastic.

Decorative hairsticks: Vintage beads and jewelry findings are threaded onto 2" head pins. A small hole is drilled into the tops of the hairsticks and the end of the head pin is glued into the hole on the end of the hairstick with industrial strength glue. (Decorative hairsticks designed by Ann Benson.)

Sachet bag: The sachet bag is made from vintage fabric and filled with potpourri, then tied closed with cording. Flea-market beads and a necklace pendant are attached to the cording for a decorative accent.

Knotted-scarf gift box: A silk scarf is wrapped around a gift box and knotted on top. Amber-colored beads are strung onto beading wire and wound around the box for a touch of elegance.

Cowboy picture pins: A 2" x 2½" cropped photograph is sandwiched between a 2" x 2½" piece of glass and a 2½" x 3" piece of 24-gauge tooling copper. The corners of the copper are cut, diagonally, to the corner of the glass, then folded up over photograph and glass to secure. Beads and charms taken from pieces of vintage western jewelry are strung onto wire, which was twisted and wrapped around the edge of the frame and soldered in place. The pinback is soldered to the back of the pin.

Beaded frame: Cabochons and beads, removed from a Southwestern-style bracelet, are used to embellish a natural wood frame. (Beaded frame designed by Ann Benson.)

Crystal drawer pulls: Sections of a vintage bracelet are glued onto the heads of screws and used as drawer pulls. The drawer pulls are then accented with vintage beads, charms, and crystal drops attached with jump rings.

Beaded and tasseled shelf: Two strands of beads, one large and one small, are draped and hung around a wall shelf. Extra beads from a vintage necklace are added to tassels and hung from the bottom decorative edges of the shelf.

Pearl-trimmed shelf: A vintage strand of pearls is attached to a metal shelf. Some portions of the necklace are re-moved, then crystals are attached and rehung as drops.

Beaded vintage crocheted collar: A chain necklace with clasp is attached to each end of a vintage crocheted collar. Beads and pieces from old earrings are glued onto the collar.

High-heeled pincushion: A single high-heeled shoe is covered with a variety of fabric and lace scraps. A piece of velvet is stuffed with batting and placed inside the shoe for a pincushion. A brooch and other jewelry findings are then glued onto the shoe, along with ribbon flowers and streamers. (High-heeled pincushion designed by Mary Jo Hiney.)

Porcelain rose necklace: Porcelain roses are washed with lavender watercolor and glued onto a gold-tone medallion that had missing beads. Assorted beads and pearls from old earrings are glued around the roses for accents. Faux teardrop pearls are washed with lavender acrylic paint and knotted onto one end of 2½" stands of purple beads. The strands are twisted together and attached to the medallion. Three strands of various sized faux pearl necklaces, lavender-washed with acrylic paint, are attached to the pendant.

Wire- and bead-trimmed gift box: A piece of 10-gauge aluminum wire is bent in half and twisted together, then a faceted gem is glued onto the bent end. Two additional pieces of wire are cut and bent around the twisted wires. Bracelet charms and beads are then strung onto the wire. The wire ends are bent into spiral shapes.

Pearl-beaded collar necklace: A beaded appliqué is removed from a vintage gown and backed with scrim. Necklace findings are attached to both ends.

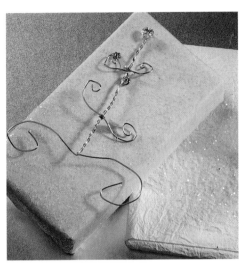

Bead and wire brooch: Beads were taken from a vintage dress, strung onto wire, and twisted together to create this intricate bead and wire brooch.

Beaded rosary: Beads from vintage necklaces are restrung onto a ¼"-wide length of satin ribbon. Knots are placed after several beads are strung, leaving small spaces of ribbon showing. A crucifix from a flea-market necklace and a Virgin Mary charm are knotted in place.

Bead and wire bookmark: Beads are threaded onto 20-gauge sterling silver wire and bent into spiral shapes. Hand-dyed variegated yarn is tied to one end and a small cross charm from a bracelet is tied to the other.

Jeweled-cross bookmark: The jeweled-cross pendant from a vintage necklace is threaded onto a gold ribbon with metallic gold edges. The two ribbon ends are knotted together with an overhand knot.

Pearls and lace bookmark: A child's wire and faux pearl bracelet is bent into the initial "C." A ¾"-wide piece of lace is tied onto the bracelet and the remaining end is knotted.

Bell-trimmed neck-lace and earrings: Tiny Christmas bells in a variety of styles, sizes, and colors are attached to a chain necklace, which looks like a piece from the 1950s, and kidney ear wires. (Bell-trimmed necklace and earrings designed by Ann Benson.)

Rose and crystal barrette: Velvet roses and ribbon flowers, removed from 1950s' hats, are glued onto a barrette which is further embellished with crystal bead drops. The crystal bead drops are created by stringing assorted crystal beads onto beading thread and stitching them onto the barrette.

Button and seed bead necklace: Colorful ⅜", flea-market buttons and seed beads are strung together with beading thread.

Heart pincushion: A cardboard heart shape is covered with a stuffed satin heart and trimmed with lace, a flea-market silver brooch, and a small charm. Beads are threaded onto a hat pin and glued in place.

Oval pincushion: This pincushion is made by covering a cardboard oval shape with batting, fabric, and lace. A crystal pendant is glued onto the center of the pincushion and accented with ribbon roses and cording. The fancy hat pins in the cushion also are made from vintage jewelry pieces.

Porcelain plate pincushion: The center of a porcelain plate was covered with a padded fabric scrap to make a pincushion. A tiny piece of cross-stitch is placed in a vintage picture brooch. An antique piece of tatting is used to cover one end of the pincushion and the brooch is pinned over it.

Beaded-necklace towel wrap (opposite page, left): A broken beaded necklace is strung onto a piece of cording. The strand is then wrapped and tied around a bath towel as a decorative element. (Beaded-necklace towel wrap designed by Linda Durbano.)

Ethnic-beaded necklace accent (opposite page, right): Bath towels are accented with a flea-market ethnic-beaded pouch necklace. (Ethnic-beaded necklace accent designed by Linda Durbano.)

Beaded-tassel towel wrap (right): Large stone and glass beads are attached to each end of a beaded necklace. The necklace is wrapped and tied around a bath and hand towel that are hung over a towel rack. (Beaded-tassel towel wrap designed by Linda Durbano.)

Jewelry-charms votives: These votive cups are made by stringing the flea-market beads and charms onto wire or thread and wrapping tightly around the upper edge of the votive cup.

Party invitations: Invitations are inserted into cardboard tubes and wrapped with decorative papers. Vintage ribbon and cording are tied around the tubes and oriental necklace charms, coins, and beads are attached.

Window charms: Chain necklaces and beaded chain necklaces are hung in a window to catch the light. Pendants, festoon pendants, charms, and a variety of crystals are hung from the ends of the necklaces.

Pearl-accented bottle: Necklace pieces and individual faux pearls are glued in a decorative design to the front of a pretty bottle, using industrial-strength glue. (Pearl-accented bottle designed by Ann Benson.)

Collecting Jewelry

Jewelry has been created and worn since earliest civilization and considered to be one of the oldest decorative art forms. Jewelry not only has monetary value, it also has sentimental worth. Because they have been carefully kept and are generally made of metals and stones, many pieces have survived throughout generations.

The styles and designs of jewelry are generally the result of the social and economic trends of the era in which it was produced. In the 1700s, precious jewelry was owned by those few who were wealthy because the pieces were hand-made and produced on a small scale. The early to mid-1800s brought about a more affluent middle class, which allowed the middle and working classes to purchase inexpensive jewelry. With the increased interest for inexpensive jewelry rising, mass production became the best way to support the demand. During the last half of the 1800s, the Arts and Crafts and Art Nouveau movements brought back the desire by artisans to singularly produce jewelry that was an art form as a reaction against mass production.

Collecting jewelry is unlike collecting antiques in other fields. Ceramics and metalworks, along with other collectibles, are generally signed or marked by the artisans that produced them. Jewelry, oftentimes, was left unmarked. One of the best ways to date jewelry is by its style. Familiarizing oneself with jewelry styles and periods, through books and museums, will be of benefit when looking for collectible jewelry.

Caring for Vintage Jewelry

When collecting jewelry, keep the following thoughts in mind:

• Antique jewelry should be treated with care since it may not have been designed for an active life-style.

• Look for signs of wear and regularly check settings for a loose stone. If caught early, a lost stone or irreparable damage may be avoided.

• Keep jewelry that you wish to preserve, especially hard stones, in separate pouches. Because of the softness of some precious metals, cut stones may scratch or damage jewelry surfaces. It also eliminates dust and other damaging influences from affecting a piece.

• Clean jewelry on a regular basis. Through wear, body oil and cosmetics can damage or discolor jewelry. Dust or tarnish may also harm collectible jewelry.

• Avoid overcleaning antique jewelry because it may remove a delicate finish that is part of the jewelry's design. Victorian jewelry typically has a fine frosted finish that could mistakenly be polished to a shine. Overcleaning fragile surfaces such as enamel or plating will wear them down.

• When having jewelry restored or repaired, seek out a reputable jeweler that has experience with antique jewelry.

• Always get a receipt when leaving jewelry with a jeweller for restoration or repair. It will provide proof that you left it with the jeweller if it becomes lost or stolen.

• When keeping jewelry as a valued collectible, it is not a good idea to replace broken or missing parts with modern replacements. The jewelry will lose value and the replacement parts may look noticeably out of place. If restoration is what you are after, it must be properly done by someone who specializes in the restoration of fine antique jewelry.

Flea Market Directory

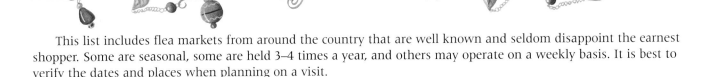

This list includes flea markets from around the country that are well known and seldom disappoint the earnest shopper. Some are seasonal, some are held 3–4 times a year, and others may operate on a weekly basis. It is best to verify the dates and places when planning on a visit.

Alabama

Birmingham Fairgrounds Flea Market
Alabama State Fairgrounds
Birmingham, AL
(800) 362-7538
First weekend of every month and three weekends in December

Collinsville Trade Day
Hwy. 11 South
Collinsville, AL
(888) 524-2536
Every Saturday

Alaska

Downtown Saturday Market
3rd and E Streets
Anchorage, AK
(907) 272-5634
Every Saturday from Memorial Day weekend through Labor Day weekend

Arizona

Shoppers Barn Swap Meet
13480 West Hwy. 84
Casa Grande, AZ
(520) 836-1934
Every Friday, Saturday, and Sunday

Fairgrounds Antique Market
Arizona State Fairgrounds
Phoenix, AZ
(800) 678-9987
Third weekend of every month, except October

Tanque Verde Swap Meet
4100 Palo Verde Road
Tucson, AZ
(520) 294-4252
Every Thursday though Sunday

Arkansas

Hot Springs Flea Market
2138 Higdon Ferry Road
Hot Springs, AR
(501) 525-9927
Daily

California

America's Largest Antique and Collectible Sale
Cow Palace
San Francisco, CA
(503) 282-0877
One weekend event in February, May, and August

Long Beach Antique & Collectible Market
Veterans Memorial Stadium
Long Beach, CA
(213) 655-5703
Third Sunday of every month

Kobey's Swap Meet at the Sports Arena
3500 Sports Arena Boulevard
San Diego, CA
(619) 226-0650
Second Sunday of every month

Outdoor Antique and Collectible Market
Long Beach Veterans Stadium
Long Beach, CA
(323) 655-5703
Third Sunday of every month

Santa Monica Outdoor Antique and Collectible Market
Santa Monica Airport
Santa Monica, CA
(213) 933-2511
Fourth Sunday of every month

The Rose Bowl
1001 Rose Bowl Drive
Pasadena, CA
(310) 587-4411
Second Sunday of every month

Trouble-Shooters Antiques and Collectibles Roundup
Cal State Fullerton
Fullerton, CA
(323) 560-7469
First Sunday in May and October

Colorado

Mile-High Flea market
7007 East 88th Avenue
Henderson, CO
(800) 861-9900
Every Wednesday, Saturday, and Sunday

The Flea Market
5225 East Platte Avenue
Colorado Springs, CO
(719) 380-8599
Every weekend, every Friday from June through September

Connecticut

Elephant Trunk Flea Market
490 Danbury Road
Mansfield, CT
(860) 456-2578
Every Sunday from early spring through Thanksgiving

Farmington Antiques Weekend
Town Road
Farmington, CT
(508) 839-9735
*Second weekend in June and
Labor Day weekend*

**Woodbury Antiques and
Flea Market**
Main Street South
Woodbury, CT
(203) 263-2841
Every Saturday

Delaware

**Spence's Auction and
Flea Market**
550 South New Street
Dover, DE
(302) 734-3441
Every Tuesday and Friday

Florida

Renninger's Twin Market
20051 Hwy. 441
Mt. Dora, FL
(904) 383-3141
*Third weekend of the month in season, with
extravaganzas in January
and February*

International Market World
1052 Hwy. 92 West
Auburndale, FL
(941) 665-0062
Every Friday, Saturday, and Sunday

Frontenac Flea Market
5605 U.S. Hwy. 1
Cocoa, FL
(407) 631-0241
Every Friday, Saturday, and Sunday

**Oakland Park Boulevard
Flea Market**
3161 West Oakland Park Boulevard
Fort Lauderdale, FL
(305) 949-7959
Every Wednesday through Sunday

Georgia

Keller's Flea Market
5901 Ogeechee Road
Savannah, GA
(912) 927-4848
Every weekend

Lakewood Antiques Market
2000 Lakewood Way
Atlanta, GA
(404) 622-4488
Second full weekend of every month

**Southeastern Antique and
Collectible Market**
Georgia National Fairgrounds
Perry, GA
(912) 471-8112
*Four weekends a year, major show
in the fall*

Scott Antique Market
Atlanta Exposition Center
I-285 at Jonesboro Road
Atlanta, GA
(614) 569-4112
Second weekend of every month

Hawaii

Aloha Flea Market
Aloha Stadium parking lot
Honolulu, HI
(808) 732-9611
Every Wednesday, Saturday, and Sunday

Illinois

**Kane County Antique and
Flea Market**
Kane County Fairgrounds
Randall Road
between Routes 38 & 64
St. Charles, IL
(708) 377-2252
One weekend a month, weekend varies

Sandwich Antiques Market
The Fairgrounds
Route 34
Sandwich, IL
(773) 227-4464
Monthly

Towanda Antique Flea Market
Towanda, IL
(309) 728-2810
July 4th

Indiana

West Washington Flea Market
6445 West Washington Street
Indianapolis, IN
(317) 244-0941
Every Friday through Saturday

Iowa

Collectors Paradise Flea Market
County Fairgrounds
What Cheer, IA 50268
(515) 634-2109
Three weekends a year

Kansas

Mid-America Flea Market
Kansas Coliseum
Wichita, KS
(316) 663-5626
One Sunday, September through June

Kentucky

The Kentucky Flea Market
Fair and Expo Center
Louisville, KY
(502) 456-2244
*Almost monthly, with several
extravaganzas*

**Lexington Antique and
Flea Market**
Lexington Center
Main and Patterson
Lexington, KY
(502) 456-2244
Eight weekends a year

Louisianna

Jefferson Flea Market
5501 Jefferson Hwy.
New Orleans, LA
(504) 734-0087
Every Friday through Sunday

Maine

Montsweag Flea Market
Route 1
Woolwich, ME
(207) 443-2809
Every weekend, May through mid-October

Maryland

Hunter's Sale Barn
Route 276
Rising Sun, MD
(410) 658-6400
Every Monday

Massachusetts

J and J Promotions Antiques and Collectibles Shows
Route 20
Brimfield, MA
(410) 658-6400
Three two-day shows, May, July, and September

Olde Hadley Flea Market
45 Lawrence Plain Road
Hadley, MA
(413) 586-0352
Every Sunday, late-August through October

Wellfleet Flea Market
Route 6
Wellfleet, MA
(508) 349-2520
Every weekend and holiday Mondays, mid-April through October

Michigan

Allegan Antique Market
Allegan County Fairgrounds
Allegan, MI
(616) 453-8780
Last Sunday, April through September

Gibraltar Trade Center North
237 North River Road
Mount Clemens, MI
(810) 465-6440
Every Friday through Sunday

Minnesota

Traders Market
I-35 and County Road
Elko, MN
(612) 461-2400
Saturday through Monday, around July 4th and Labor Day

Mississippi

First Monday Trade Days
Hwy. 15
Ripley, MS
(601) 837-7442
Ripley, MS
First Monday of every month and preceding weekend

Missouri

Frison Flea Market
7025 St. Charles Rock Road
St. Louis, MO
(314) 727-0460
Every Friday through Sunday

New Hampshire

Grandview Flea Market
Junction of Route 28 and 28 Bypass
Derry, NH
(603) 432-2326
Every weekend

New Jersey

Collingwood Auction and Flea Market
State Highways 33 and 34
Collingwood Park, NJ
(732) 938-7941
Every Friday through Sunday

New Egypt Auction and Farmers Market
Route 537
New Egypt, NJ
(609) 758-2082
Every Wednesday and Sunday

New Mexico

Fairgrounds Flea Market
State Fairgrounds
Albuquerque, NM
(505) 265-1791
Every weekend, except September

Trader Jack's Flea Market
Flea Market Road
Santa Fe, NM
(505) 382-9404
Every weekend

New York

Bouckville Antiques Pavillion
Rte. 20
Bouckville, NY
(315) 893-8972
Sundays, May through October, extravaganzas in June and August

Mulford Farm Antique Show and Sale
Main St. and James Lane, East Hampton, NY
(516) 537-0333
One Saturday a month, June, August, and September

Stormville Airport Antique show and Flea Market
Stormville Airport,
Rte. 216
Stormville, NY
(914) 221-6561
One weekend a month, April through October

The Annex Antiques Fair & Flea Market
(26th Street Market)
Sixth Avenue, between 25th and 26th Streets
New York, NY
(212) 243-5342
Every weekend

North Carolina

Metrolina Exposition Flea Market
7100 Statesville Road
Charlotte, NC
(704) 596-4643
First and third weekend of every month, a spectacular the first weekend of April, June, November

Starway Flea market
2346 Carolina Beach Road
Wilmington, NC
(910) 763-5520
Every Friday through Saturday

North Dakota

Magic City Flea Market
State Fairgrounds
Minot, ND
(701) 852-1289
Fourteen weekends yearly, except January

Ohio

Scott Antique Market
Expo Center
717 East 17th Avenue
Columbus, OH
(614) 569-4112
*One weekend a month, generally
the third weekend*

Springfield Antique Show
& Flea Market
Clark County Fairgrounds
Exit 59 off I70
Springfield, OH
(937) 325-0053
*Extravaganzas one weekend in
March and October*

Oklahoma

AMC Flea Market
1001 North Pennsylvania Avenue
Oklahoma City, OK
(405) 232-5061
Every weekend

Oregon

Picc-a-dilly Flea Market
Lane County Fairgrounds
Eugene, OR
(541) 683-5589
Sundays, September through June

Portland Antique Show
Exposition Center
2060 North Main Street
Portland, OR
(503) 282-0877
Weekends in March, July, October

Pennsylvania

Renninger's #2 Antique Market
740 Noble Street
Kutztown, PA
(570) 385-0104
*Every Saturday, three two-day extravaganzas
in April, June, and September*

Schupp's Grove
Adamstown, PA
(717) 484-4115
Weekends, April through October

Rhode Island

Rocky Hill Flea Market
Rocky Hill Fairgrounds
East Greenwich, RI
(401) 884-4114
Every Sunday, April through November

South Carolina

Anderson Jockey Lot and
Farmers Market
Hwy. 29
Anderson, SC
(864) 224-2027
Every weekend

Coastal Carolina Flea Market
Hwy. 78
Ladson, SC
(843) 797-0540
Every weekend

South Dakota

Black Hills Flea Market
5500 Mount Rushmore Road
Rapid City, SD
(605) 343-6477
One weekend, May through September

Tennessee

Crossville Flea Market
Hwy. 70 North
Crossville, TN
(931) 484-9970
One weekend, May through September

Heart of Country
Opry Land Hotel
2800 Opry Land Drive
Nashville, TN
(800) 862-1090
One weekend in February and October

Texas

First Monday Trade Days
290 East Tyler
Canton, TX
(903) 567-6556
*The week preceding the first Monday
of each month*

Round Top
Round Top, TX
(281) 493-5501
*Semiannual show, first weekend of
April and October*

Vermont

The Original Newfane Flea Market
Route 30
Newfane, VT
(802) 365-4000
*Every Sunday, mid-April through
mid-November*

Virginia

VFW Flea Market
VFW Complex
Hillsville, VA
(703) 728-7188
*Annually, Labor Day and the preceding
Friday through Sunday*

Washington, D.C.

Flea Market at Eastern Market
Seventh Street S.E.
Washington, D.C.
(703) 534-7612
*Every Sunday from March through
Christmas, except May*

West Virginia

Harpers Ferry Flea Market
Route 340
Harpers Ferry, WV
(304) 725-0092
*Every Sunday from mid-March
through October*

Wisconsin

Maxwell Street Days
Field Park
Mukwonago, WI
(414) 363-2003
*Second weekend in June and September,
third weekend in July and August*

Metric Equivalency Chart

mm-millimetres   cm-centimetres
inches to millimetres and centimetres

inches	mm	cm	inches	cm	inches	cm
⅛	3	0.3	9	22.9	30	76.2
¼	6	0.6	10	25.4	31	78.7
⅜	10	1.0	11	27.9	32	81.3
½	13	1.3	12	30.5	33	83.8
⅝	16	1.6	13	33.0	34	86.4
¾	19	1.9	14	35.6	35	88.9
⅞	22	2.2	15	38.1	36	91.4
1	25	2.5	16	40.6	37	94.0
1¼	32	3.2	17	43.2	38	96.5
1½	38	3.8	18	45.7	39	99.1
1¾	44	4.4	19	48.3	40	101.6
2	51	5.1	20	50.8	41	104.1
2½	64	6.4	21	53.3	42	106.7
3	76	7.6	22	55.9	43	109.2
3½	89	8.9	23	58.4	44	111.8
4	102	10.2	24	61.0	45	114.3
4½	114	11.4	25	63.5	46	116.8
5	127	12.7	26	66.0	47	119.4
6	152	15.2	27	68.6	48	121.9
7	178	17.8	28	71.1	49	124.5
8	203	20.3	29	73.7	50	127.0

Index

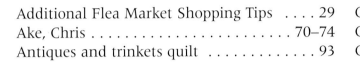